BAND

SI ONLINE

Multimedia Resources for
TEACHERS
STUDENTS
PARENTS

SOUND INNOVATIONS

for CONCERT BAND

A Revolutionary Method for Beginning Musicians

Robert **SHELDON** | Peter **BOONSHAFT** | Dave **BLACK** | Bob **PHILLIPS**

Congratulations on deciding to be a member of the band!

This book is here to help you get started on a very exciting time in your life. When you complete Book 1, you'll be well prepared to play many types and styles of music. Playing in the band will bring you years of incredible experiences.

Maybe you'll make music an important part of your life by attending concerts, playing in a community band, and supporting the arts. Maybe you'll pursue a career in music as a performer, teacher, composer, sound engineer, or conductor. Whatever you choose, we wish you the best of luck in becoming a part of the wonderful world of music.

Correlated Sound Innovations media will help you practice and develop new skills. Video lessons and audio demonstration tracks reinforce good technique and musical accuracy, and PDFs provide supplemental tunes, exercises, lessons, and assessment pages. Visit the *SI Online* resource site for access:

SIOnline.alfred.com

SI ONLINE

Multimedia Resources for
TEACHERS
STUDENTS
PARENTS

 Audio demonstration and accompaniment tracks are included for every line of music in the book.

 Video demonstrations of fundamental skills and exercises are included. Look for the video icon throughout this book.

 Supplemental enrichment content and additional repertoire for practice and reinforcement are available to download at SIOnline.alfred.com.

Visit the *SI Online* resource site to stay up to date with newly added content.
SIOnline.alfred.com

alfred.com

ISBN-10: 0-7390-6727-3 (Book & Online Media)
ISBN-13: 978-0-7390-6727-7 (Book & Online Media)

Instrument photos courtesy of Yamaha Corporation of America Band & Orchestral Division
Audio recorded and mixed at The Lodge Recording Studios, Indianapolis, IN
Bass clarinet performance in audio recordings by Greg Imboden
Accompaniments written and recorded by Derek Richard
Ensembles performed by American Symphonic Winds, Anthony Maiello, Conductor

Production Company: Specialized Personnel Locators
Engineer: Kendall S. Thomsen
Video filming and production: David Darling, Grand Haven, MI
Bass clarinet artist in video: Alcides Rodriguez

Ready? Set? Play!

Sound advice for getting started on your instrument

▶ *Instrument Assembly*
▶ *Disassembly & Cleaning*

1. YOUR INSTRUMENT—PARTS OF THE BASS CLARINET

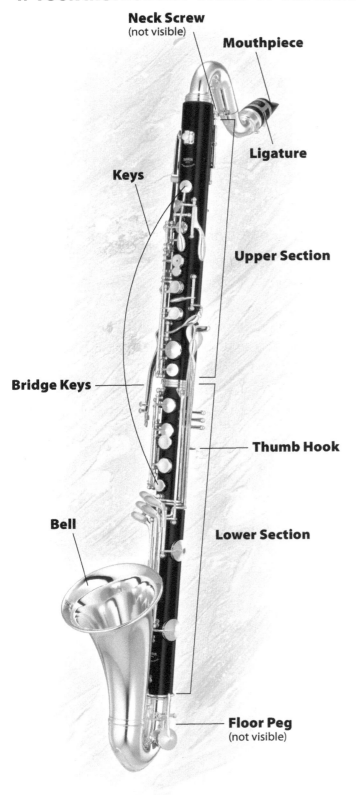

Neck Screw
(not visible)

Mouthpiece

Ligature

Keys

Upper Section

Bridge Keys

Thumb Hook

Bell

Lower Section

Floor Peg
(not visible)

2. PUTTING IT ALL TOGETHER

A. Place the thin end of the reed into your mouth to moisten it.

B. When needed, place a small amount of cork grease on each cork. Clean your hands after applying.

C. Some bass clarinets have one long body section while others have the upper and lower sections separated. If your instrument is separated, carefully lift the upper section with your left hand and the lower section with your right hand. With the upper section keys depressed, gently twist the sections together being careful to align the bridge keys and avoid bending them.

D. Carefully lift the bell, depress the key and gently twist it into place being careful to align the key.

E. Some bass clarinets use a neckstrap while others use a floor peg. If your bass clarinet uses a neckstrap, place it over your head, so the hook is in the front and the pad is resting on the back of your neck.

F. Place the hook of the neckstrap into the ring on the back of the bass clarinet or adjust the floor peg to the proper height.

G. Rest the instrument on your lap and steady it with your left hand.

H. Gently twist the neck into position and tighten the neck screw.

I. Remove the mouthpiece cap and ligature. Gently twist the mouthpiece onto the neck. Be sure the flat part of the mouthpiece is facing down.

I. Add the ligature to the mouthpiece, then slide the thick end of the reed against the mouthpiece with the flat side against the rectangular opening. The reed should be centered and not extend above the top of the mouthpiece. Gently tighten the ligature screws to hold the reed in place.

3. PUTTING IT ALL AWAY

A. Remove the ligature and reed from the mouthpiece.

B. Place the reed in a reed guard. This helps it dry properly and last longer.

C. Disassemble in reverse order of assembly. Use the swab to dry the inside of the instrument from the neck. Wipe off the outside with a soft cloth. Carefully place the instrument in the case and close all the latches.

D. Store only your instrument and its accessories in the case. Music, folders and other objects may bend keys and damage the instrument.

First Sounds

POSTURE AND PLAYING POSITION

A. Sit on the front edge of the chair.

B. Keep feet flat on the floor.

C. Sit tall with your back straight.

D. With the bell centered between your legs, adjust the neckstrap or floor peg, so the mouthpiece falls comfortably into your mouth with your head kept at a level position.

E. Place your right thumb under the thumb rest near the base of the thumbnail.

F. The left thumb will cover the thumb key and the pads of your fingers will press the keys or tone holes.

G. Keep fingers relaxed and naturally curved as if holding a ball.

EMBOUCHURE

A. Your mouth position (or embouchure) is an important part of creating a good sound.

B. Moisten your lips and roll your lower lip over your teeth to cushion the reed.

C. Place the reed and mouthpiece on your lower lip, so it extends about three-quarters of an inch into your mouth.

D. Rest your upper teeth on the top of the mouthpiece.

E. Tighten your mouth around the mouthpiece keeping the corners firm and chin relaxed and down.

BREATHING

A. Take a full breath by inhaling deeply through your mouth

B. Exhale gently and completely.

C. Neck and shoulders should be relaxed. Shoulders should not move, but your waist should expand with each breath in.

PLAYING YOUR FIRST SOUNDS

A. Assemble the mouthpiece (reed and ligature attached) to the neck.

B. Form your embouchure around the mouthpiece.

C. Take a deep, full breath through the corners of your mouth.

D. Touch your tongue gently against the reed and exhale quietly as you say "too." Hold the note as long as possible.

E. Play several sounds on one breath by saying, "tee, tee, tee" or "too, too, too" as you exhale. This is called "tonguing" since you are using your tongue to start the new sound.

EQUIPMENT NEEDS

A. Always keep several reeds in your case stored in reed guards. Reeds play best after they have been used for at least an hour. Take turns playing on two or three reeds by using a different reed each day, so you always have a good reed for playing your best. Discard broken, chipped or cracked reeds.

B. Reed guards allow reeds to dry thoroughly between uses and protect them from damage when not being played.

C. Keep a cleaning swab, soft cloth, mouthpiece cap and cork grease in your case for maintaining your instrument.

▶ *Posture*

▶ *Holding the Instrument*

▶ *Embouchure & First Sounds*

▶ *Breathing*

▶ *Reeds*

▶ *Corks, Pads & Screws*

▶ *Tonguing*

Sound Notation

Music has its own language and symbols that are recognized worldwide.

TIME SIGNATURE
(or **METER**)
Indicates the number of beats (counts) in each measure and the type of note that receives one beat

BAR LINE
Divides the staff into measures

MEASURE
The distance between two bar lines

LEDGER LINE
Extends the staff either above or below

STAFF
5 lines and 4 spaces used for writing music

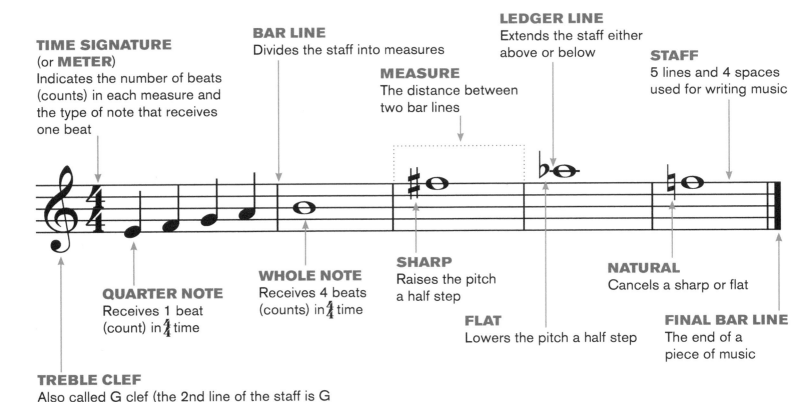

SHARP
Raises the pitch a half step

FLAT
Lowers the pitch a half step

NATURAL
Cancels a sharp or flat

FINAL BAR LINE
The end of a piece of music

QUARTER NOTE
Receives 1 beat (count) in 4/4 time

WHOLE NOTE
Receives 4 beats (counts) in 4/4 time

TREBLE CLEF
Also called G clef (the 2nd line of the staff is G and the clef is drawn by first circling the G line)

Locating note names on the staff:

LINES

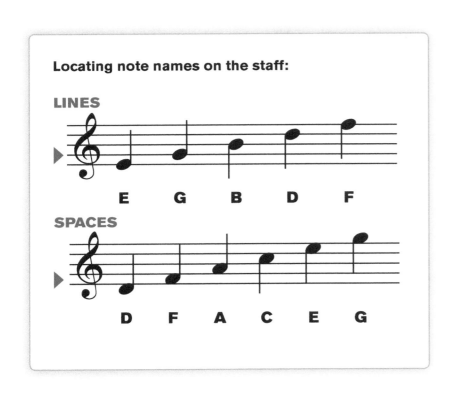

E   G   B   D   F

SPACES

D   F   A   C   E   G

HOW TO PRACTICE

As you play through this book, some parts will be very easy while others may require more time to play well. Practicing your instrument every day will help you achieve excellence. Carefully play each exercise until you can perform it comfortably three times in succession.

▶ Practice in a quiet place where you can concentrate.

▶ Schedule a regular practice time every day.

▶ Use a straight back chair and a music stand to assist you in maintaining good posture.

▶ Start each practice session by warming up on low notes and long tones.

▶ Focus on the music that is most difficult to play, then move on to that which is easier and more fun.

▶ Use your recordings to help you play in tune and in time.

▶ *A Good Tone*

◀)) **1** *Listen to the note and match the pitch. This is the first note you learn on page 5.*

Level 1: Sound Beginnings ▶ *First Five Notes*

The **TREBLE CLEF** (G Clef) identifies the location of notes on the staff. The tail of the treble clef circles the G on the staff. G is on the 2nd line.

A **TIME SIGNATURE** or **METER** indicates the number of beats (counts) in each measure and the kind of note that receives one beat.

4/4 TIME is a meter in which there are 4 beats per measure and the quarter note receives 1 beat.

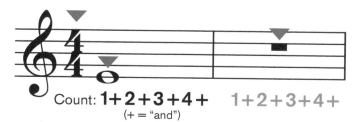

Count: **1 + 2 + 3 + 4 +** 1 + 2 + 3 + 4 +
(+ = "and")

WHOLE NOTES receive 4 beats (counts) in 4/4 time.

WHOLE RESTS indicate a full measure of silence.

OUR FIRST NOTE *Introducing the new note, E.*

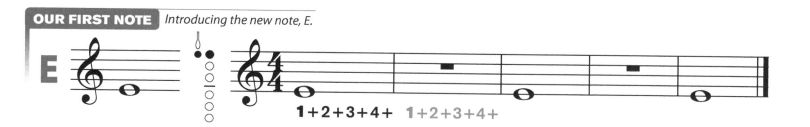

1 + 2 + 3 + 4 + 1 + 2 + 3 + 4 +

OUR SECOND NOTE *Introducing the new note, D.*

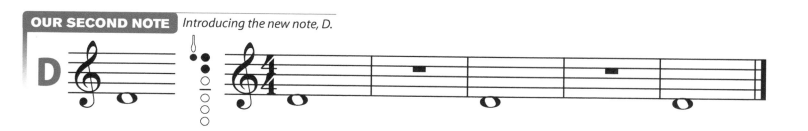

TWO-NOTE TANGO—*Practice going from one note to the other.*

OUR THIRD NOTE *Introducing the new note, C.*

6

THREE-NOTE COMBO—*Practice playing all three notes.*

6

THIRD TIME'S THE CHARM—*Additional practice on these three notes.*

7

A **SOLO** is when one person is performing alone or with accompaniment.

MATCH THE PITCH—*Play the solo part as the rest of the band answers with the same note. Take turns with other band members.*

8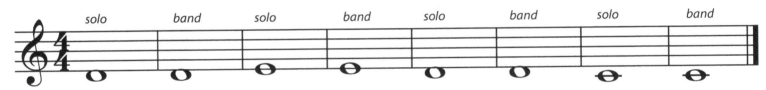

The **BREATH MARK** tells you to take a deep breath through your mouth.

A BREATH OF FRESH AIR—*Name each note before you play.*

9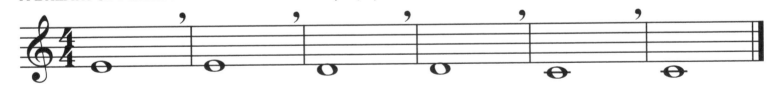

BREATHING EASY—*Sing the notes, then play.*

10

THREE-ZY DOES IT!—*Practice playing three different notes in a row.*

11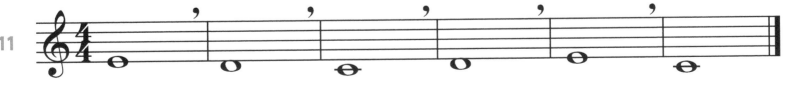

HALF NOTES receive two beats (counts) in 4/4 time.

HALF RESTS receive two beats (counts) of silence and look similar to whole rests. Since half rests only contain two beats, they are "light" and therefore float above the line. Because most whole rests contain an entire measure of beats, they are "heavier" and therefore sink below the line.

The REPEAT SIGN tells you to go back to the beginning and play the piece again.

HALF THE TIME—*Introducing half notes and half rests. Repeat as indicated. Clap the rhythm as you count the beats, then sing the piece before you play.*

MIX IT UP—*Play each group of half notes in one breath while changing notes.*

A **DUET** is a composition for two performers. When both parts are played together, you will sometimes hear two different notes played at the same time which creates **HARMONY**.

DUET? DO IT!—*Introducing our first duet.*

NAME THE NOTES—*Write the name of each note in the space provided, then sing the notes before you play.*

8

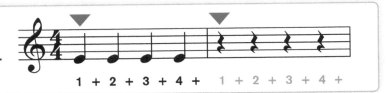

QUARTER NOTES receive one beat (count) in 4/4 time.
QUARTER RESTS receive one beat (count) of silence.

1 + 2 + 3 + 4 +   1 + 2 + 3 + 4 +

QUARTER NOTES—*Introducing quarter notes and quarter rests. Play each group of notes in one breath. Count, clap and sing before you play.*

16

1 + 2 + 3 + 4 +   1 + 2 + 3 + 4 +

QUARTERLY REPORT—*Name each note before you play.*

17

A **PHRASE** is a musical idea that ends with a breath.

HOT CROSS BUNS—*Play the phrase, not just the notes!*

English Folk Song

18

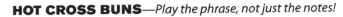

OUR FOURTH NOTE *Introducing the new note, F.*

19

F

SCALING THE WALL—*Practice using your newest note. Breathe only at the breath marks and rests.*

20

OUR FIFTH NOTE *Introducing the new note, G.*

21

G

SCALING NEW HEIGHTS—*Practice using another new note.*

22

MERRILY WE ROLL ALONG—*Breath marks help define the phrases.*

Traditional

AU CLAIRE DE LA LUNE—*More phrase and note practice. Add breath marks to create your own musical phrases.*

French Folk Song

COMMON TIME is another name for the $\frac{4}{4}$ time signature and is indicated with this symbol:

A **FERMATA** tells you to hold a note or rest longer than its normal duration.

A **COMPOSER** is a person who writes music. Look for the composer's name on the upper right corner of the music.

Who wrote the music to *Jingle Bells*?

JINGLE BELLS—*Play this piece in common time and notice the* fermata *at the end. Count, clap and sing before you play.*

James Lord Pierpont

1 + 2 + 3 + 4 +

GO TELL AUNT RHODY—*More practice in common time with a fermata.*

American Folk Song

LIGHTLY ROW—*Play this duet in common time. Switch parts on the repeat.*

Traditional

TUTTI tells you that everyone plays together.

GOOD KING WENCESLAS—*The soloist and full band take turns playing.*

Traditional English Carol

A **ROUND** is a type of music in which players start the piece at different times, creating interesting harmonies and accompaniments.

SWEETLY SINGS THE DONKEY (round)—*Play this round by having players or groups start every four measures. This piece continues on the next staff, which does not need to show the meter.*

American Folk Song

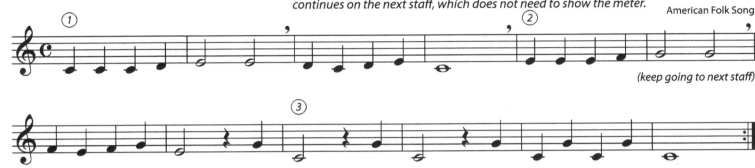

(keep going to next staff)

FERMATAS 'R US—*Your teacher will indicate how long to hold each fermata.*

DREYDL, DREYDL—*Here is a holiday song that uses all the notes you have learned.*

Traditional Hanukkah Song

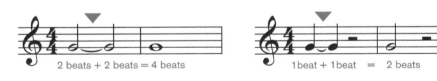

A **TIE** is a curved line that connects two or more notes of the same pitch. The tied notes are played as one longer note with the combined value of both notes.

2 beats + 2 beats = 4 beats   1 beat + 1 beat = 2 beats

A **WARM-UP** is an important part of your daily preparation. Focus on producing a beautiful sound.

A **CHORALE** is a harmonized melody played slowly. Many bands play chorales as part of their warm-up.

WARM-UP CHORALE—*Play with a beautiful sustained tone. Listen for the harmony!*

TIE AND TIE AGAIN—*Play the tied notes full value. This piece can be played as a duet along with the* Warm-Up Chorale.

▶ Complete the **SOUND CHECK** near the end of your book.

Level 2: Sound Fundamentals

OUR SIXTH NOTE *Introducing the new note, A.*

TWINKLING STARS—*Play this familiar melody using your new note.*

Adapted by Wolfgang Amadeus Mozart

(keep going to the next staff)

JOLLY OLD ST. NICK—*Here is a duet that uses your new note.*

Traditional Carol

New Time Signature (Meter) 2/4 TIME

2 = Two beats (counts) per measure.
4 = A quarter note receives one beat (count).

RHYTHMS IN 2/4—*Clap the rhythm while counting the beats aloud.*

1 + 2 + 1 + 2 + 1 + 2 + 1 + 2 +

TWO-FOUR OUT THE DOOR—*This exercise has two beats per measure. Count, clap and sing before you play.*

1 + 2 + 1 + 2 +

LONDON BRIDGE—*Here's a melody you know in 2/4 time. How many beats does the last note receive?*

English Folk Song

TWO-FOUR OLD MAC—*Name each note before you play.*

Traditional

TECHNIQUE BUILDER—*Practice slowly at first, then gradually get faster each time you play.*

40

SOUNDS NEW! *Introducing the new note, low B.*

41

MARY ANN—*This calypso (Caribbean dance) tune uses your new note. Notice the long ties over the bar lines. Discuss with your teacher the characteristics of music in different styles. Listen to the recording of this piece and describe this style of music.*

Caribbean Folk Song

42

CONDUCTORS lead groups of musicians using specific hand and arm patterns.

Conduct the ²⁄₄ pattern with your right hand.

(conductor's view)

REHEARSAL MARKS are reference numbers or letters in a box above the staff. They are also called *rehearsal numbers* or *letters*. They help musicians find logical places to start and stop when learning the piece.

POLLY WOLLY DOODLES—*Take turns conducting the band.*

American Folk Song

43

DUET OF THE CRUSADERS—*This duet uses your new high and low notes.*

German Folk Song

44

SHOO-FLY!—*This melody features ties across the bar line.*

American Folk Song

ON THE BRIDGE AT AVIGNON—*Sing the note names, then take turns conducting the band as they play.*

French Folk Song

SOUND THEORY—*Draw a clef, meter (hint: look at the last note), bar lines and a final bar line. Write the names of the notes and number of beats for each note before you play.*

Number of beats: 2   1   1   __ __ __ __ __ __ __ __ __ __

Note Names: E   F   F   __ __ __ __ __ __ __ __ __ __

DIVISI (div.) indicates where two notes appear at the same time. Each note should be played by an equal number of players to achieve a balanced harmony.

UNISON (unis.) indicates where two parts play the same note.

WARM UP—*Play with a beautiful sound and listen to the harmony on the divided notes!*

The **KEY SIGNATURE** appears at the beginning of the staff. It tells you which notes will be played sharp or flat. Different instruments play in different keys. This is your key of **C MAJOR (CONCERT B-FLAT)**, with no sharps or flats.

MARCHING MADNESS—*Full band arrangement.*

March tempo

ROCK THIS BAND!—*Full band arrangement.*

50 Hard rock

EIGHTH NOTES each receive a half beat (count) in 4/4 time. Two eighth notes receive one count. Eighth notes often appear in pairs or in groups of four and have a *beam* across the note stems.

1 +

1 + 2 + 3 + 4 +

51 **RHYTHM ROUND-UP**—*Clap the rhythm as you count the beats.*

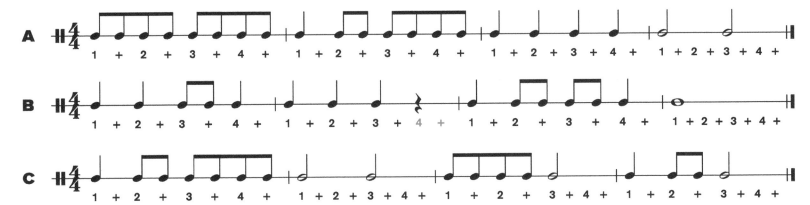

52 **GOTTA HAND IT TO YA! (Clapping Duet)**—*Clap either Part A or B, then switch parts on the repeat.*

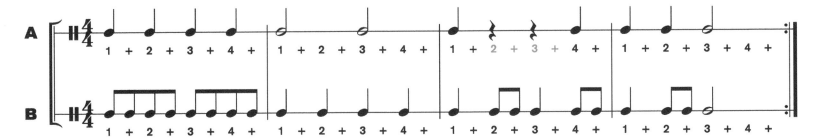

PIECES OF EIGHT—*Count the rhythm first, clap, then play.*

53

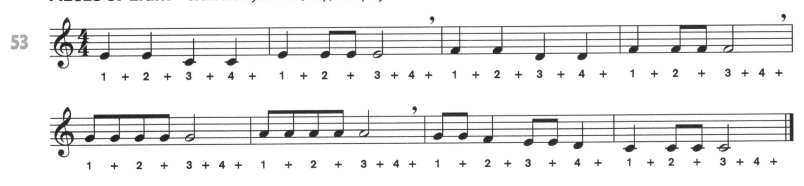

DYNAMICS in music refer to the change in volume you create when playing loud or soft. Italian terms are often used in music. The term we use for loud is **FORTE** and is indicated by the letter f, and the term we use for quiet (or soft) is **PIANO** and is indicated by the letter p.

WHISPER AND SHOUT!—*Play the notes with the dynamics indicated.*

(look ahead to the next line for the dynamic change)

LONG, LONG AGO—*Play this familiar melody with dynamics.*

Thomas Haynes Bayly

(the f carries over to this line)

SKIP TO MY LOU—*More fun with dynamics! Name each note before you play.*

American Folk Song

DYNAMIC DUET—*Read the dynamics carefully as they are different in each part. Switch parts on the repeat.*

THIS OLD MAN—*Here is a tune to play just for fun!*

American Folk Song

16

An **INTERVAL** is the distance between two notes. The interval of an 8th is called an **OCTAVE**.
The interval on the same note is a **UNISON**.

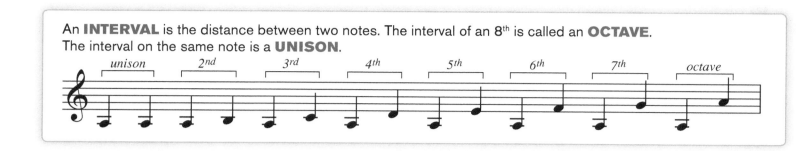

SOUNDS NEW! *Introducing the new note, low A.*

59

INTERESTING INTERVALS—*Build your technique. Write the name of each interval in the space provided before you play.*

60

Interval: 2nd   _____   _____   _____   _____   _____   _____   _____ _____ _____

HEY, HO! NOBODY'S HOME—*Practice dynamics.*

English Folk Song

61

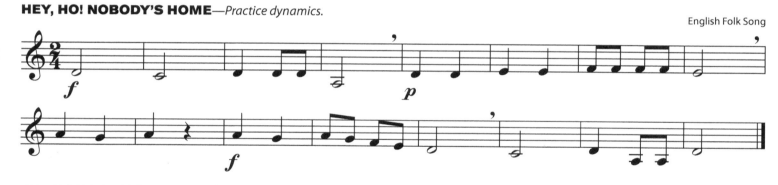

A **CRESCENDO** (*cresc.* or ———◁)
tells you to gradually play louder.

A **DECRESCENDO** or **DIMINUENDO**
(*decresc., dim.* or ▷———) tells you to gradually play softer.

TURN THE VOLUME UP—*Increase your airstream to create a louder sound.*

62

TURN THE VOLUME DOWN—*Reduce your airstream to create a softer sound. For extra fun, play this with* Turn the Volume Up *as a duet.*

63

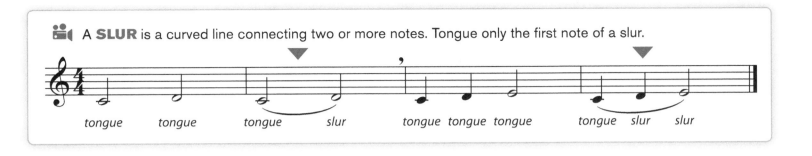

A **SLUR** is a curved line connecting two or more notes. Tongue only the first note of a slur.

tongue   tongue   tongue   slur   tongue tongue tongue   tongue slur slur

FRÈRE JACQUES (round)—*Practice the slurs in this familiar melody, then play it as a round.*

French Folk Song

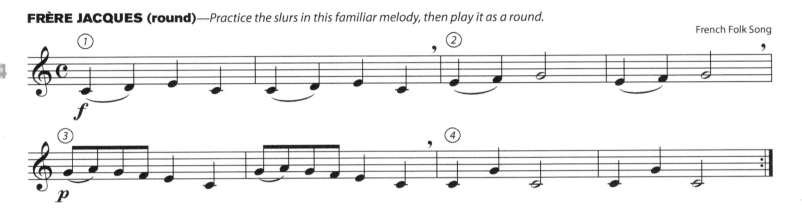

PICKUP NOTES occur before the first complete measure of a phrase. Often the last measure of the piece will be missing the same number of beats as the pickup notes have.

4 +   1 + 2 + 3 + 4 +   1 + 2 + 3 +

A TISKET, A TASKET—*How many beats are in the pickup?*

American Folk Song

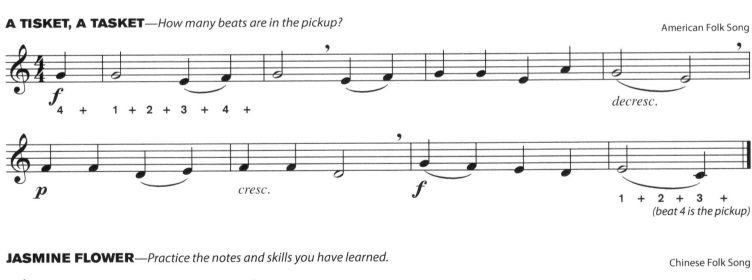

decresc.

4 + 1 + 2 + 3 + 4 +

cresc.   *f*

1 + 2 + 3 +
(beat 4 is the pickup)

JASMINE FLOWER—*Practice the notes and skills you have learned.*

Chinese Folk Song

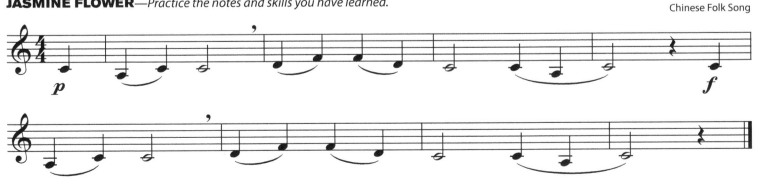

18

ERIE CANAL—*How many beats are in the pickup? How many beats are missing from the last measure?*

Thomas S. Allen

67

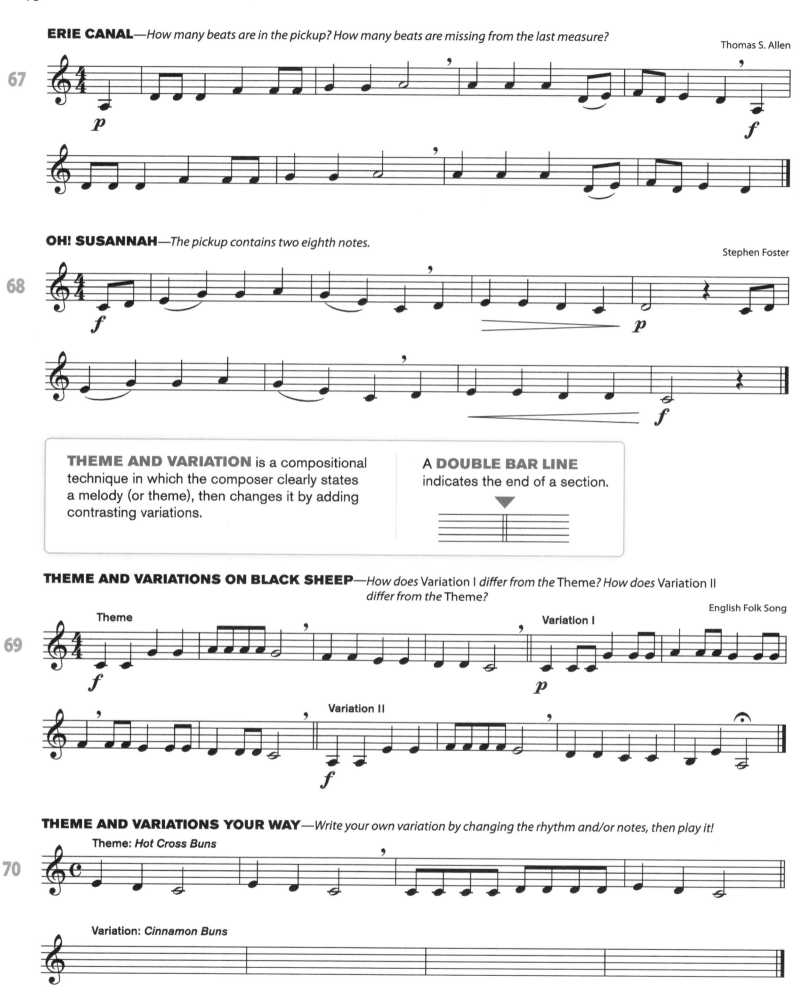

OH! SUSANNAH—*The pickup contains two eighth notes.*

Stephen Foster

68

THEME AND VARIATION is a compositional technique in which the composer clearly states a melody (or theme), then changes it by adding contrasting variations.

A **DOUBLE BAR LINE** indicates the end of a section.

THEME AND VARIATIONS ON BLACK SHEEP—*How does* Variation I *differ from the* Theme? *How does* Variation II *differ from the* Theme?

English Folk Song

69

Theme

Variation I

Variation II

THEME AND VARIATIONS YOUR WAY—*Write your own variation by changing the rhythm and/or notes, then play it!*

70

Theme: *Hot Cross Buns*

Variation: *Cinnamon Buns*

TEMPO MARKINGS indicate the speed of the music.

LARGO is a slow tempo.
ANDANTE is a moderate walking tempo.
ALLEGRO is a fast tempo.

Conduct the $\frac{4}{4}$ pattern with your right hand.

Conduct each piece below at the correct tempo.

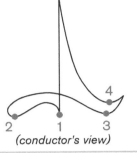

(conductor's view)

Austrian composer **Wolfgang Amadeus Mozart** (1756–1791) was one of the most influential musicians of the Classical period. Though he only lived to the age of 35, he was very prolific and is known for his symphonies, operas, chamber music and piano pieces.

German-born composer **Johannes Brahms** (1833–1897) was one of the leading figures of the Romantic period in music history. Brahms is best known for his four symphonies, two piano concertos and his remarkable choral work *A German Requiem*.

SERENADE—*Full band arrangement.*

Wolfgang Amadeus Mozart

INVADERS!—*Full band arrangement. Remember, in $\frac{2}{4}$ time a whole measure rest receives two beats.*

ACADEMIC FESTIVAL OVERTURE—*Full band arrangement.*

Johannes Brahms

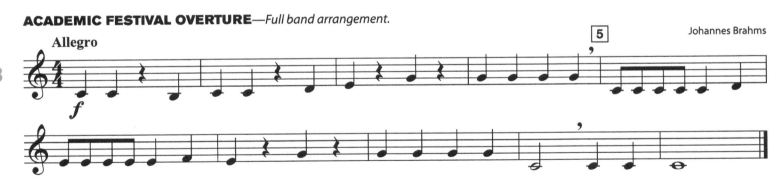

STODOLA PUMPA—*Practice good posture and breathing skills.*

Czech Folk Song

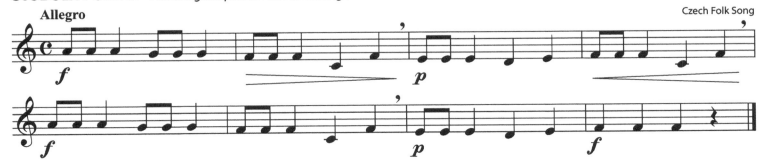

More dynamics! **MEZZO FORTE** (*mf*) is medium loud. **MEZZO PIANO** (*mp*) is medium soft.

DYNAMITE DYNAMICS—*Review all four of the dynamics you've learned, along with crescendo and decrescendo.*

Stephen Collins Foster (1826–1864), best known for composing songs such as *Beautiful Dreamer*, *Oh! Susanna* and *Camptown Races*, is often called "the father of American music" and the "first professional songwriter."

MY OLD KENTUCKY HOME—*Solo with piano accompaniment.*

▶ Complete the **SOUND CHECK** near the end of your book.

Level 3: Sound Musicianship

SOUNDS NEW! *Introducing the new note, B♭.*

The new key signature of **F MAJOR** (concert E-flat) tells you that all B's are flat.

STYLE MARKINGS are sometimes used instead of tempo markings to help musicians understand the feeling the composer would like the music to convey.

WAY UP HIGH—*Before you play, circle all the notes affected by the key signature. Discuss ways in which you can make this sound "sweet."*

Sweetly

BINGO—*Before playing, discuss ways in which you can make this sound "light." Name the key.*

Lightly   American Folk Song

1ˢᵀ AND 2ᴺᴰ ENDINGS: Play the 1ˢᵗ ending the first time through. Repeat the music, but skip over the 1ˢᵗ ending on the repeat and play the 2ⁿᵈ ending instead.

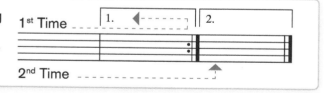

BUFFALO GALS—*Since this is played with spirit, the tempo should be energetic! Watch the 1ˢᵗ and 2ⁿᵈ endings.*

With spirit!   American Traditional

MUSETTE—*Here is a tune to play just for fun!*

Andante   Johann Sebastian Bach

¾ TIME is a meter in which there are 3 beats per measure and the quarter note receives 1 beat.

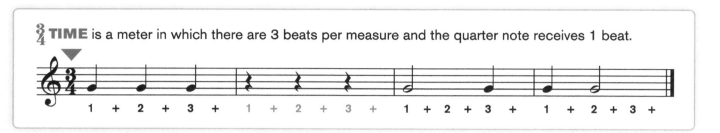

1 + 2 + 3 + 1 + 2 + 3 + 1 + 2 + 3 + 1 + 2 + 3 +

MEXICAN HAT DANCE—*Write the number of each beat you play in the space provided. Count, clap and sing before you play.*
See how well your performance of Mexican Hat Dance *captures the style of a dance.*

Mexican Folk Song

Allegro

82

mf   1   2   3

1.   2.

A **DOT** increases the length of a note by half its value. Since a half note receives 2 counts, the dot that follows receives 1 count. Therefore, a **DOTTED HALF NOTE** receives 3 beats in both ¾ and ⁴⁄₄ time.

1 + 2 + 3 + 1 + 2 + 3 + 1 + 2 + 3 + 1 + 2 + 3 +

BARCAROLLE—*Name the key. Look for the breath marks to help you phrase and play this in a gentle style.*
Try memorizing this melody and playing it expressively.

Jacques Offenbach

Gently

83

1 + 2 + 3 +
mp

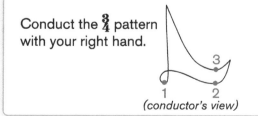

Conduct the ¾ pattern with your right hand.

3

1   2

(conductor's view)

Edvard Grieg (1843–1907) was a Norwegian composer and pianist of the Romantic period. He is best known for his *Piano Concerto in A minor* and his wonderful *Peer Gynt Suite*, which includes the famous *In the Hall of the Mountain King* and *Morning.*

MORNING—*Before you play, sing and conduct the following piece.* Moderato *is a medium tempo.*

Moderato

Edvard Grieg

84

mf

SOUNDS NEW! *Introducing the new note, low B♭.*

An **ACCIDENTAL** is a ♯, ♭, or ♮ sign placed in front of a note to alter its pitch. The effect lasts until the end of the measure. Determine how the key signatures, accidentals and bar lines affect the notes in the following exercise.

TWO-NOTE TREAT

Name the key: ____   *Name the key:* ____   *(the accidental is still in effect)*

Name these notes: ____   ____   ____ ____

A **RIGHT-FACING REPEAT** shows where to begin repeating the music.

TRAP-EAZY DOES IT!—*Before you play, think about the repeats.*

Gaston Lyle

Andante

mf

1.   2.

SOUNDS NEW! *Introducing the new note, low G.*

G

TAKE NOTE—*What does* Largo *mean?*

Largo

mf

THE CARNIVAL OF VENICE—*Here is another melody with a pickup note and 1st and 2nd endings.*

Italian Folk Song

Moderato

f

1.   2.

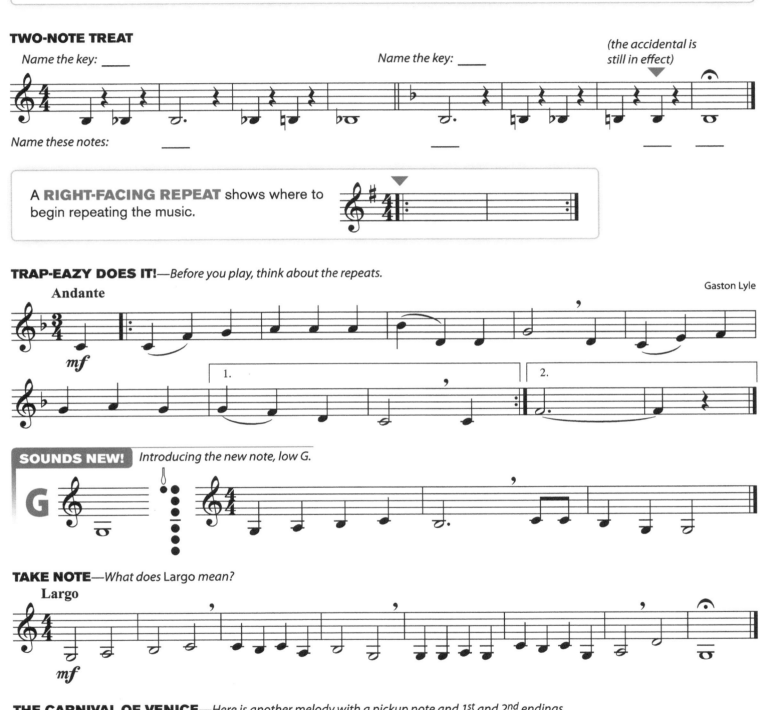

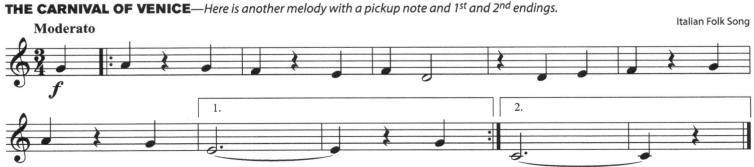

An **ARTICULATION** indicates the way a note should be played. An **ACCENT** is an articulation that tells you the note should be played with a stronger attack.

CHESTER—Chester *was often referred to as the "unofficial anthem" of the American Revolution.*

Proudly

William Billings

91

A **ONE-MEASURE REPEAT** means to play the previous measure again.

EIGHTH NOTES and **EIGHTH RESTS** are not always in pairs. They can be single notes and rests. Single eighth notes have a flag on the stem rather than a beam.

MARCHING ALONG—*Circle the accents and the one-measure repeat before you play.*

Moderate march tempo

92

93 **EXERCISES ON EIGHTHS**—*Demonstrate your understanding of eighth notes and rests by clapping these exercises. Switch parts on the repeat.*

94 **EMPHASIS ON ACCENTS**—*Try both parts of this clapping duet and be sure to clap louder on the accented notes. Before you play, circle the single eighth notes and eighth rests in Part B.*

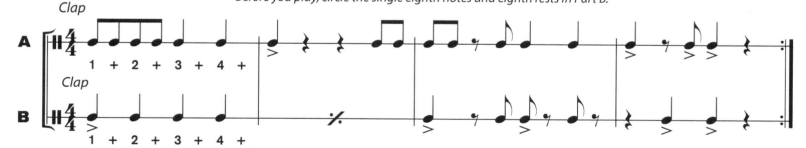

EMPHASIS ON NOTES—*Now play the accents by using more air to make the accented notes louder.*

Andante

95

DOWN BY THE STATION—*Practice eighth notes, slurs and accents.*

American Folk Song

96

BROTHER JOHN (round)—*More practice using articulations (slurs and accents) and one-measure repeats, then play it as a round.*

French Folk Song

97

SOUNDS NEW! *Introducing the new note, F♯.*

98

The new key signature of **G MAJOR** (concert F) tells you that all F's are sharp.

BREATHING: Breath marks have been included so far to show you where to breathe. Now you can determine this yourself by finding logical places to take a breath, such as during rests and at the end of a phrase.

AURA LEE—*How does this new key signature affect the notes you will play?*

George R. Poulton

99

SAKURA—*This melody has a right-facing repeat. Before you play, trace your finger over the "roadmap" of the piece.*

Japanese Folk Song

100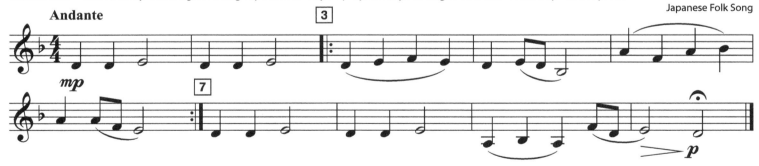

SHE WORE A YELLOW RIBBON—*Here's a tune to play just for fun!*

George A. Norton

101

A quarter note receives 1 beat, and the dot that follows receives ½ a beat, therefore, a **DOTTED QUARTER NOTE** receives 1½ beats and can be subdivided into three eighth notes. (♩. = ♪♪♪)

Count and clap, then play this rhythm. Notice that the quarter note tied to the eighth sounds the same as the dotted quarter note.

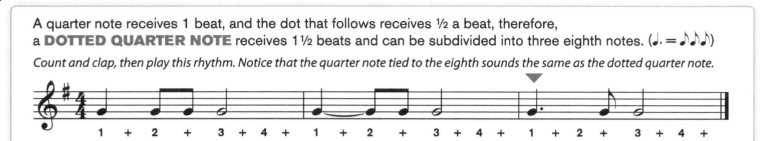

A WHOLE LOTTA TIES—*Feel the pulse of the beat on the tied eighth note.*

Moderato

102

A WHOLE LOTTA DOTS—*Feel the pulse of the beat on the dot.*

Moderato

103

D.C. AL FINE indicates to repeat from the beginning and play to the **FINE** (the end).

Antonín Leopold Dvořák (1841–1904) was a Czech composer of the Romantic period best known for drawing inspiration from folk music and for his remarkable *New World Symphony* and *Slavonic Dances*.

THEME FROM THE "NEW WORLD SYMPHONY"—*Play the D.C., then end at the Fine.*

Antonín Dvořák

Largo

104

SYNCOPATION occurs when there is emphasis on a weak beat.

JOY TO THE WORLD—*Full band arrangement.*

Joyfully

Christmas Carol

105

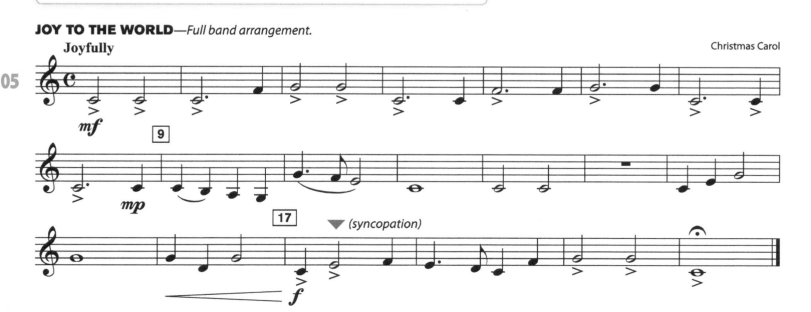

COURTESY ACCIDENTALS help remind you of the key signature. They usually occur after another accidental or a recent key change. These special accidentals are enclosed in parentheses.

ACCIDENTAL ENCOUNTERS—*Before you play, name all the notes.*

(notice the key signature change)

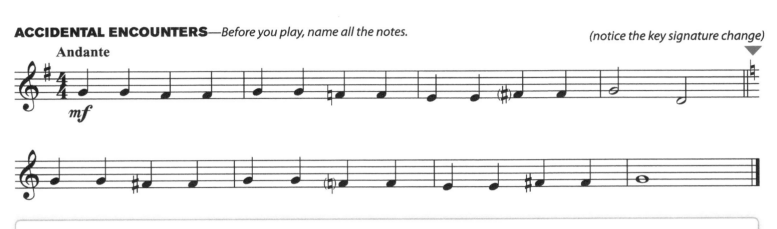

D.S. AL FINE indicates to repeat from the sign (𝄋) and play to the *Fine*.

German composer **Ludwig van Beethoven** (1770–1827), despite losing his hearing, composed a vast number of works including string quartets and concertos. He is best known for his nine symphonies, especially his renowned *Fifth Symphony*.

ODE TO JOY—Maestoso *means to play majestically. Circle the "sign" then clap, count and sing before you play.*

Ludwig van Beethoven

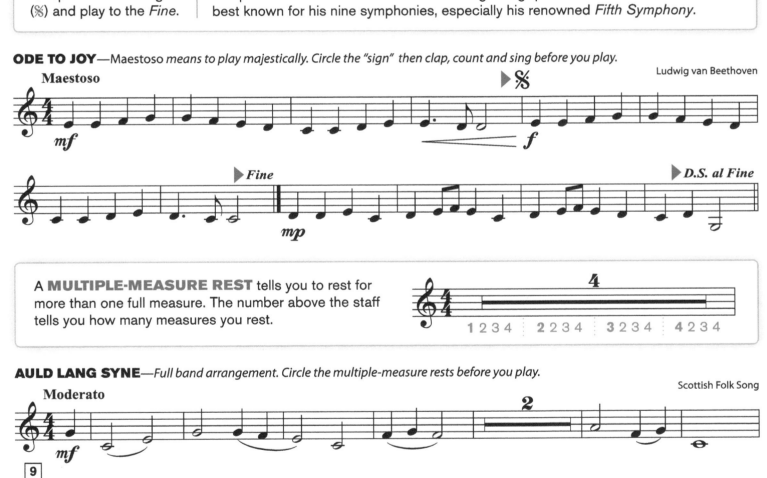

A **MULTIPLE-MEASURE REST** tells you to rest for more than one full measure. The number above the staff tells you how many measures you rest.

AULD LANG SYNE—*Full band arrangement. Circle the multiple-measure rests before you play.*

Scottish Folk Song

MICHAEL, ROW THE BOAT ASHORE—*Always play with a beautiful sound.*

African-American Spiritual

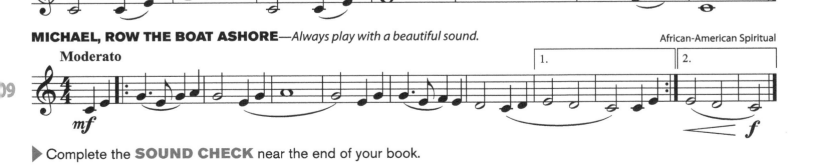

▶ Complete the **SOUND CHECK** near the end of your book.

Level 4: Sound Development

A **SCALE** is a series of notes that ascend or descend stepwise (consecutive notes) within a key. The lowest and the highest notes of the scale are always the same letter name and are an octave apart.

A **WALTZ** is a popular dance in 3/4 time.

CONCERT B♭ MAJOR SCALE (YOUR C MAJOR SCALE)—*Memorize this scale!*

110

THREE-FOUR, PHRASE SOME MORE—*This melody starts with a phrase that sounds as if it asks a question, followed by a phrase that sounds as if it provides the answer. Play this as a duet with the Concert B♭ scale.*

111

DOWN THE ROAD—*Play with a steady stream of fast air.*

NEW NOTE! *Introducing the new note, low F.*

112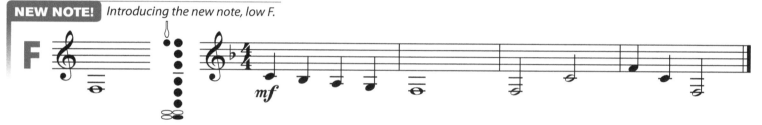

SUO GAN—*Play this melody in the style of a lullaby.*

Welsh Folk Song

113

LEGATO (–) is an articulation or style of playing that is smooth and connected. It is indicated by a line.

STACCATO (·) is an articulation or style of playing that is light and separated. It is indicated with a dot.

ARTICULATION STATION—*Play the notes with the indicated articulation.* ▶ *Articulation Station: Accents, Staccato, and Legato*

114

OVERTURE TO "WILLIAM TELL"—*Here is a familiar tune that uses* legato *and* staccato.

Gioacchino Rossini

115

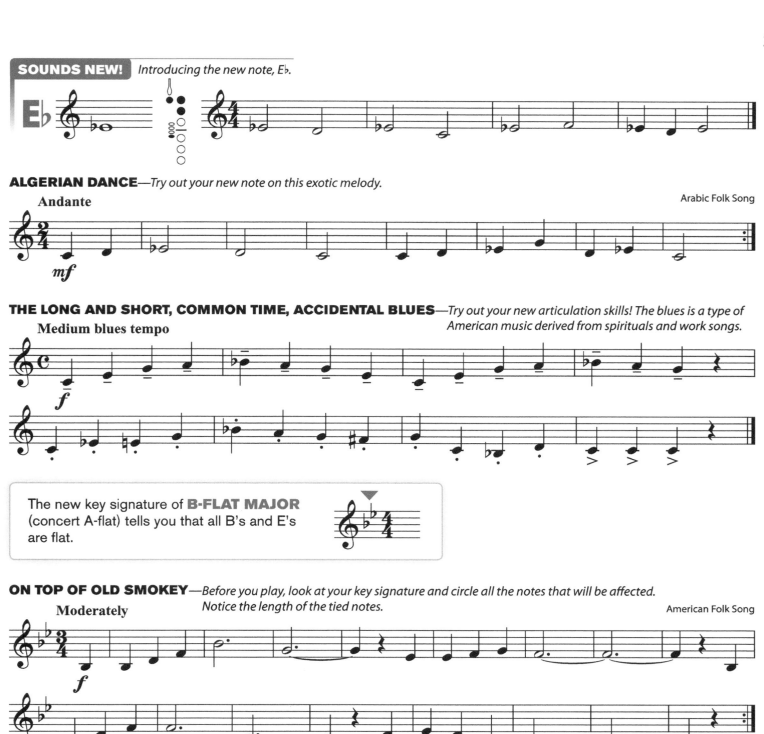

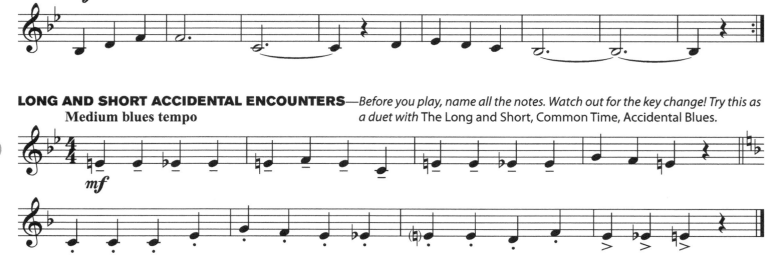

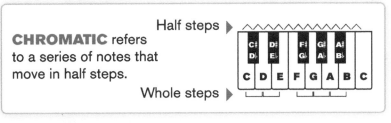

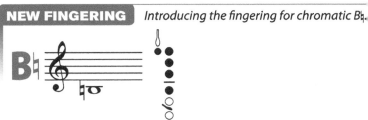

CHROMATIC MARCH—*Try out your half-stepping skills! Find the courtesy accidental. Alla marcia tells us to play in the style of a march.*

(use chromatic B♮ fingering)

123   **JAZZ DOO-ETTE**—*Play this piece in the style of the "jazz big bands" popular in the 1930s and 1940s. Name the key.*

ON YOUR OWN!—*Play the first four measures, then write the last four measures yourself! Now, play the entire piece.*

MUSIC MY WAY! Write your own composition:
- Write in the clef, meter, key signature, tempo and style you choose.
- Place the notes and rhythms that you already know on the staff in any order you like and add a final bar line.
- Add articulations (staccato, legato, accents, slurs) and dynamics (***p***, ***mp***, ***mf***, ***f***, *cresc.*, *decresc.*).
- Give the piece a title, and be sure to add **YOUR NAME** as the composer.
- Now play the piece for your friends and family!

Title: _____   Composed by _____

CAN-CAN—*Vivo means lively and spirited!*

Jacques Offenbach

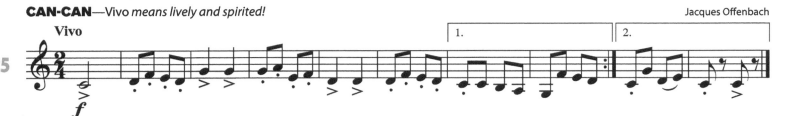

VOLGA BOAT SONG—Pesante *means to play in a heavy style. Memorize this piece and play in an expressive manner.*

Russian Folk Song

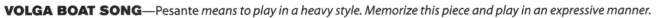

With your teacher, develop a list of rules for good concert etiquette. Some things to include might be to listen quietly and to show your appreciation by applauding at the end of the piece. Take turns performing *All Through the Night* while others in your class practice good concert etiquette.

ALL THROUGH THE NIGHT—*Name the key.*

Welsh Folk Song

ARIRANG—*Name the key. Discuss with your teacher the characteristics of music from different cultures. Listen to the recording of this piece and describe those characteristics.*

Korean Folk Song

MINUET—*A minuet is a French country dance.*

Johann Sebastian Bach

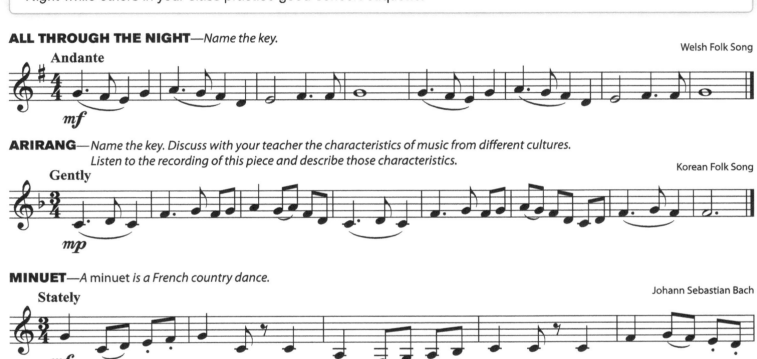

Take turns performing *Sailor's Chantey* while other members of the class evaluate the performance using criteria developed with your teacher. Consider rhythm, intonation, tone, dynamics, phrasing and expression.

SAILOR'S CHANTEY—*Name the key.*

Sea Chantey

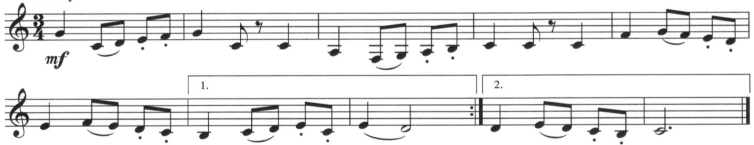

THEME FROM SWAN LAKE—*Always play with expression.*

Pyotr Il'yich Tchaikovsky

Most of the music we hear is either in a **MAJOR** key or a **MINOR** key. The sound of these keys is created by the arrangement of half steps and whole steps. The mood of a major key is often cheerful or heroic, while a minor key may be sad or solemn.

MAJOR MACARONI (YANKEE DOODLE)—*This is in a major key. How does this make you feel?*

American Traditional

MINOR MACARONI—*This is in a minor key. How does this make you feel? How is it different from Major Macaroni?*

ALOUETTE—*Is this in a major or minor key?*

French-Canadian Folk Song

HATIKVAH—*Does this sound like a major or minor key?*

Israeli National Anthem

MARCH SLAV—*Is this in a major or minor key?*

Pyotr Il'yich Tchaikovsky

▶ Complete the **SOUND CHECK** near the end of your book.

Level 5: Sound Techniques

Use the **REGISTER KEY** to play upper register notes (above 3rd line Bb). Keep your air stream fast and steady, your embouchure firm, and your chin down. Roll the thumb up just far enough to open the register key.

An **INTERLUDE** is a short musical piece. The following *Imperative Interludes* will help you learn your upper-register notes.

RANGE ROVER 1

NEW NOTE! *Introducing the new note, high E.*

▶ *Crossing the Break*

(add register key)

IMPERATIVE INTERLUDE 1

RANGE ROVER 2

NEW NOTE! *Introducing the new note, high F.*

(add register key)

IMPERATIVE INTERLUDE 2

RANGE ROVER 3

NEW NOTE! *Introducing the new note, high G.*

(add register key)

IMPERATIVE INTERLUDE 3

HIGH FLYING—*Here's a tune to play just for fun!*

Andante

mf

RANGE ROVER 4

144

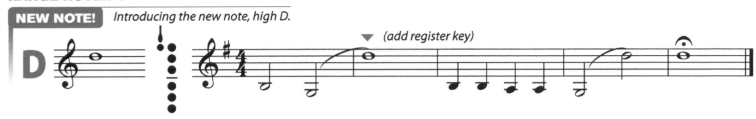

IMPERATIVE INTERLUDE 4

145

RANGE ROVER 5

146

IMPERATIVE INTERLUDE 5

147

RANGE ROVER 6

148

IMPERATIVE INTERLUDE 6

149

DRINK TO ME ONLY WITH THINE EYES—*Practice your slurs with this familiar tune.*

Traditional English Song

150

IT'S RAINING, IT'S POURING—*Play this familiar melody with a beautiful sound.*

English Folk Song

Moderato

mf

IT'S WINDY, IT'S STORMING—*Try playing this piece as a duet with* It's Raining, It's Pouring.

Moderato

mf

RANGE RIDER

NEW NOTE! *Introducing the new note, low E.*

E

CRAZY FINGERS

Moderato

mf

RANGE ROVER 7

NEW NOTE! *Introducing the new note, high B.*

B

▼ *(add register key)*

IMPERATIVE INTERLUDE 7

SWORD DANCE—*Here's a tune to play just for fun!*

Traditional

Vivo

f

1.

2.

BREAK UP—*Practice crossing the break (moving from one register to another). Play the phrase, not just the notes.*

(keep RH [right hand] fingers down starting on A to help cross the break)

158
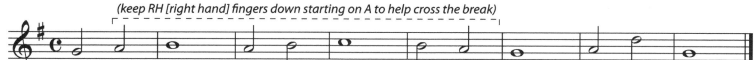

BREAK DOWN—*More practice over the break. Play with a steady stream of fast air.*

(keep RH fingers down)

159

DOWN AND OUT—*This exercise crosses the break between registers moving down stepwise from higher notes. Play with a full sound.*

Moderato

(keep RH fingers down)

160

UP AND OVER—*This exercise crosses the break between registers moving up stepwise from lower notes. Demonstrate good posture.*

Moderato

(keep RH fingers down)   *(keep RH fingers down)*   *(keep RH fingers down)*

161

THE CONCERT B♭ MAJOR SCALE (YOUR C MAJOR SCALE)—*Memorize the following ascending and descending scale.*

162

(keep RH fingers down)

An **ARPEGGIO** is the 1st, 3rd, 5th and 8th notes of the scale.

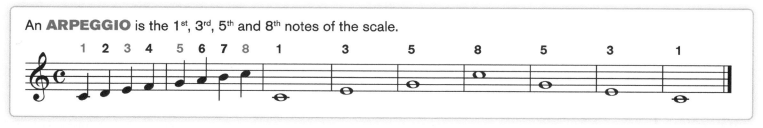

COUNTRY GARDENS—*Name the key. Before you play, notice how loud the crescendo becomes.*

Allegro

English Folk Song

163

CAMPTOWN RACES—*Before you play, notice how soft or loud each dynamic change becomes.*

Lively

Stephen Foster

164

WHEN THE SAINTS GO MARCHING IN—*Full band arrangement.*

American Gospel Hymn

Austrian composer **Franz Joseph Haydn** (1732–1809) was one of the most important composers of the Classical period. He is best known for his many symphonies, string quartets, masses, and his oratorios *The Creation* and *The Seasons*.

SURPRISE SYMPHONY—*This piece includes a "surprise" created by dynamics. Can you find the big surprise? Discuss with your teacher the characteristics of music written during this period. Listen to the recording of this piece and describe those characteristics.*

Franz Joseph Haydn

HALF-STEP HASSLE—*Practice your chromatic skills.*

HILARIOUS HALF STEPS—*Here is another chromatic challenge. Name the notes before you play.*

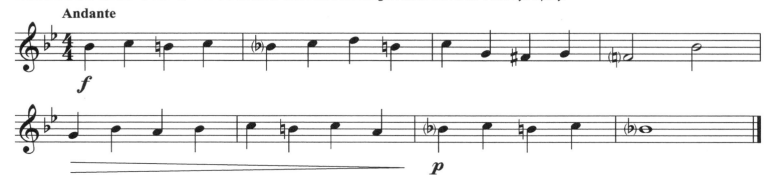

SYMPHONIC THEME FROM SYMPHONY NO. 1—*Is this a major or minor key?*

Gustav Mahler

169

An **ETUDE** is a "study" piece, or an exercise that helps you practice a specific technique.

ETUDE—*This exercise helps you become more comfortable with your chromatic notes.*

170

German composer and organist **Johann Sebastian Bach (1685–1750)** is considered to be one of the greatest composers of all time. He lived during the Baroque era and is best known for his cantatas, many works for organ, *Magnificat, St. John Passion* and *St. Matthew Passion*.

Modest Petrovich Mussorgsky (1839–1881) was a Russian composer who often used his country's history and folklore to inspire his compositions, such as *Boris Godunov, Night on Bald Mountain* and *Pictures at an Exhibition*, which includes *The Great Gate of Kiev*.

CHORALE—*Full band arrangement. Is this a major or minor key?*

Johann Sebastian Bach

171

A **RALLENTANDO** or **RITARDANDO** is an indication that the tempo is supposed to become gradually slower. It is indicated with the abbreviation *rall.* or *rit.*

THE GREAT GATE OF KIEV—*Full band arrangement.* Pictures at an Exhibition *represents a tour through an art gallery. In addition to form and color, music uses many of the same concepts as the visual arts.*

Modest Mussorgsky

172

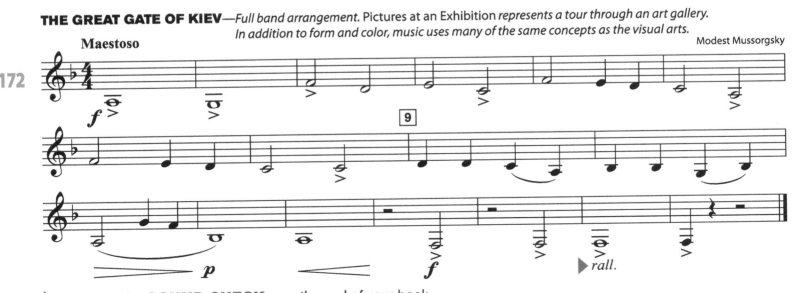

▶ Complete the **SOUND CHECK** near the end of your book.

Level 6: Sound Performance

A **SOLO** is a piece that is performed alone or with accompaniment. Before playing this piece, watch and listen to it being performed online.

SOLO: SCARBOROUGH FAIR—*This solo has a piano accompaniment.*

Traditional English Ballad

Piano Accompaniment

174 **THE BLUE-TAIL FLY (duet)**—*Switch parts on the repeat.*

American Minstrel Song

> A **TRIO** is a composition in which three different parts are played by three performers at the same time.

Many factors go into creating a great performance. Develop a list of things you think a performer should do to prepare for a performance. You might include such things as being on time, being prepared and practicing.

175 **MOLLY MALONE (trio)**—*Learn all three parts.*

Traditional Irish Ballad

TIME TRIALS—*Count and clap this exercise before you play. This piece reviews all the meters you have learned.*

176

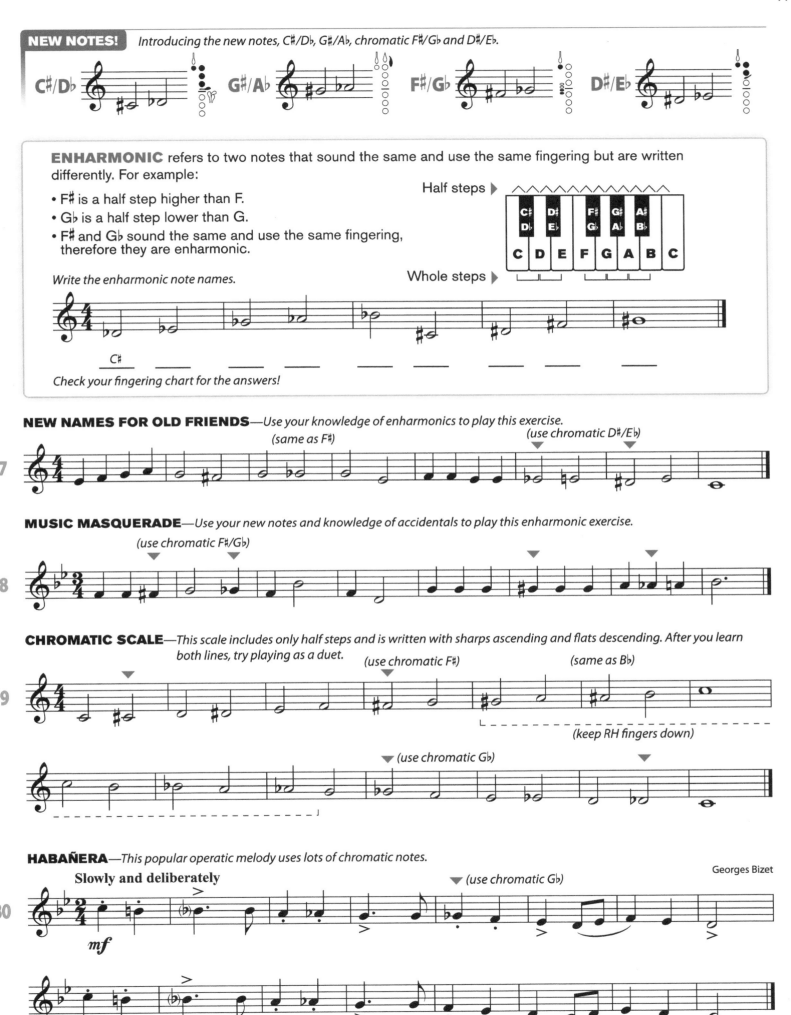

NEW NOTES! *Introducing the new notes, C#/Db, G#/Ab, chromatic F#/Gb and D#/Eb.*

ENHARMONIC refers to two notes that sound the same and use the same fingering but are written differently. For example:

- F# is a half step higher than F.
- Gb is a half step lower than G.
- F# and Gb sound the same and use the same fingering, therefore they are enharmonic.

Half steps ▶

Whole steps ▶

Write the enharmonic note names.

C#

Check your fingering chart for the answers!

NEW NAMES FOR OLD FRIENDS—*Use your knowledge of enharmonics to play this exercise.*

(same as F#)   (use chromatic D#/Eb)

77

MUSIC MASQUERADE—*Use your new notes and knowledge of accidentals to play this enharmonic exercise.*

(use chromatic F#/Gb)

78

CHROMATIC SCALE—*This scale includes only half steps and is written with sharps ascending and flats descending. After you learn both lines, try playing as a duet.*

(use chromatic F#)   (same as Bb)

79

(keep RH fingers down)

(use chromatic Gb)

HABAÑERA—*This popular operatic melody uses lots of chromatic notes.*

Georges Bizet

Slowly and deliberately   (use chromatic Gb)

80

mf

42

O CANADA—*This is the Canadian National Anthem. Play this in four-measure phrases by breathing after the long notes.*

Calixa Lavallée

181

GRANT US PEACE (round)—*Play this well-known round with the full band or as a trio.*

Traditional

182

TAKE A RIDE ON THE BLUES TRAIN—*Full band arrangement. Choose from the notes provided and make up a part as you play.*
This is called **IMPROVISATION**. *Your director will indicate when it is your turn to improvise.*

183

▶ Complete the **SOUND CHECK** near the end of your book.

Scales, Arpeggios, Warm-Up Chorales and Etudes*

Key of G Major (Concert F Major)

SCALE & ARPEGGIO

CHORALE IN CONCERT F MAJOR—*Full band arrangement.*

SCALE ETUDE

INTERVAL ETUDE

Key of C Major (Concert B♭ Major)

SCALE & ARPEGGIO

CHORALE IN CONCERT B♭ MAJOR—*Full band arrangement.*

SCALE ETUDE

INTERVAL ETUDE

*Scale and Etude exercises may be played with other instruments but are not always in unison.

Key of F Major (Concert E♭ Major)

SCALE & ARPEGGIO

192

CHORALE IN CONCERT E♭ MAJOR—*Full band arrangement.*

193

SCALE ETUDE

194

INTERVAL ETUDE

195

Key of B♭ Major (Concert A♭ Major)

SCALE & ARPEGGIO

196

CHORALE IN CONCERT A♭ MAJOR—*Full band arrangement.*

197

SCALE ETUDE

198

INTERVAL ETUDE

199

Rhythm Studies

ETUDE #1

ETUDE #2

ETUDE #3

ETUDE #4

ETUDE #5

Sound Check

Level 1
Check off each skill you have mastered.

___ Posture

___ Instrument assembly

___ New rhythms

___ Hand position

___ New notes

___ Fermata

Level 2
Check off each skill you have mastered.

___ Conducting in $\frac{2}{4}$ and $\frac{4}{4}$ time

___ Playing p and f

___ New notes

___ Slurs

___ New rhythms

___ Breathing skills

Level 3
Check off each skill you have mastered.

___ Conducting in $\frac{3}{4}$ time

___ Repeats

___ Playing mp and mf

___ Accents

___ New notes

___ Pickup notes

Level 4
Check off each skill you have mastered.

___ Legato

___ Composing a piece of music

___ Identifying major and minor keys

___ Staccato

___ Understanding concert etiquette

___ D.C. al Fine

Level 5
Check off each skill you have mastered.

___ Playing a scale

___ Rallentando or ritardando

___ Playing in a variety of styles

___ Arpeggio

___ New notes

___ Crescendo and decrescendo (or diminuendo)

Level 6
Check off each skill you have mastered.

___ Playing a solo

___ Enharmonics

___ Improvisation

___ Playing ensembles

___ Chromatic scale

___ Playing rounds

Glossary

1st and 2nd endings – play the 1st ending the first time through; repeat the music, but skip over the 1st ending on the repeat and play the 2nd ending instead

accent $(>)$ – play the note with a strong attack

accidentals $(\sharp, \flat, \natural)$ – *see page 4*

alla marcia – play in the style of a march

allegro – a fast tempo

andante – a moderate walking tempo

arpeggio – the notes of a chord played one after another

articulation – indicates how a note should be played

bass clef – indicates the fourth line of the staff is F

breath mark – tells you to take a deep breath through your mouth

chromatics – a series of notes that move in half steps

conductor – leads groups of musicians using specific hand and arm patterns

courtesy accidentals – help remind you of the key signature; occur after another accidental or recent key change; enclosed in parentheses

crescendo – gradually play louder

D.C. al Fine – repeat from the beginning and play to the *Fine*

D.S. al Fine – repeat from the sign ($\%$) and play to the *Fine*

decrescendo or diminuendo – gradually play softer

divisi – indicates where two notes appear at the same time

dot – increases the length of a note by half its value

double bar line – indicates the end of a section

duet – a composition for two performers

dynamics – change in volume

enharmonic – refers to two notes that sound the same and use the same fingering but are written differently

etude – a "study" piece, or an exercise that helps you practice a specific technique

fermata – hold a note or rest longer than its normal duration

Fine – the end of a piece of music

forte (f) – play loudly

harmony – two or more notes played at the same time

improvisation – creating music as you play

interlude – a short musical piece

interval – the distance between two notes

key signature – appears at the beginning of the staff, and indicates which notes will be played sharp or flat

largo – a slow tempo

ledger line – short, horizontal line used to extend the staff either higher or lower

legato $(-)$ – an articulation or style of playing that is smooth and connected

mezzo forte (mf) – medium loud

mezzo piano (mp) – medium soft

moderato – a medium tempo

multiple-measure rest – indicates more than one full measure of rest; the number above the staff indicates how many measures to rest

octave – the interval of an 8th

one-measure repeat $(\%)$ – play the previous measure again

phrase – a musical idea that ends with a breath

piano (p) – play softly

pickup note – occurs before the first complete measure of a phrase

rallentando – becoming gradually slower

rehearsal mark – reference number or letter in a box above the staff

repeat sign – go back to the beginning and play the piece again

right-facing repeat – indicates where to begin repeating the music

ritardando – becoming gradually slower

round – music in which players start the piece at different times, creating interesting harmonies and accompaniments

scale – a series of notes that ascend or descend stepwise within a key; the lowest and highest notes of the scale are always the same letter name and are an octave apart

slur – a curved line connecting two or more notes; tongue only the first note in a slur

solo – when one person is performing alone or with accompaniment

staccato $(\cdot)$ – an articulation or style of playing that is light and separated

style marking – sometimes used instead of a tempo marking to help musicians understand the feeling the composer would like the music to convey

syncopation – occurs when there is emphasis on a weak beat

tempo markings – indicate the speed of the music

theme and variation – a compositional technique in which the composer clearly states a melody (theme), then changes it by adding contrasting variations

tie – a curved line that connects two or more notes of the same pitch; the tied notes are played as one longer note with the combined value of both notes

time signature or meter – indicates the number of beats (counts) in each measure and the type of note that receives one beat

treble clef – indicates the second line of the staff is G

trio – a composition in which three different parts are played by three performers at the same time

tutti – everyone plays together

unison – two or more parts play the same note

waltz – a popular dance in $\frac{3}{4}$ time

Bass Clarinet Fingering Chart

○ = open
● = pressed down

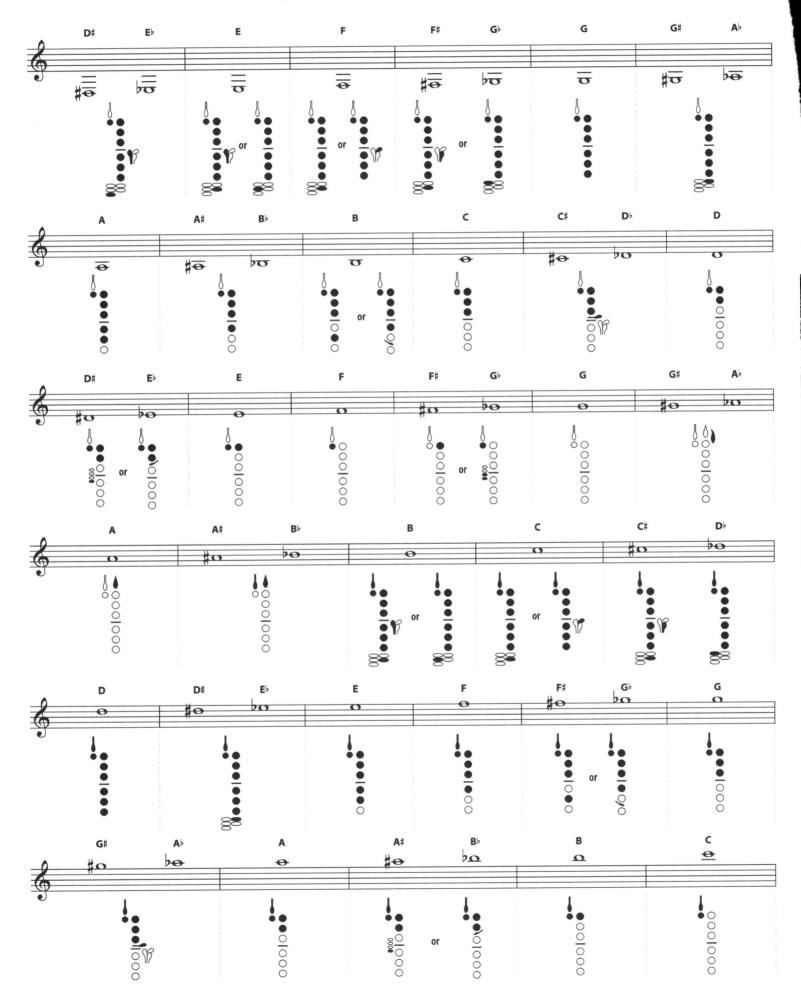